Mandala Patterns Coloring Book

Copyright: Published in the United States by Peter Raymond
Published October 2016
ISBN-13: 978-1539493679
ISBN-10: 1539493679

All rights reserved. No part of this publication may be reproduced, stored in retrieval system, copied in any form or by any means, electronic, mechanical, photocopying, recording or otherwise transmitted without written permission from the publisher. Please do not participate in or encourage piracy of this material in any way. You must not circulate this book in any format. **Peter Raymond** *does not control or direct users' actions and is not responsible for the information or content shared, harm and/or actions of the book readers.*

Thank you

www.ingramcontent.com/pod-product-compliance
Lightning Source LLC
Chambersburg PA
CBHW080621190526
45169CB00009B/3257